MACRAMè
FOR
BEGINNERS

"From basic knots to beautiful home decorations:

Stress-free projects everyone can do".

Table of Contents

Introduction: "Discovering the Art of Macramé – Your Journey Begins Here" 1
Chapter 1: Getting Started with Macramé 3
Chapter 2: Mastering the Basics of Knots 9
Chapter 3: Exploring Macramé Styles 19
Chapter 4: Helpful Techniques and Shortcuts 27
Chapter 5: Macramé for Relaxation and Mindfulness 32
Chapter 6: Inspiring Macramé Projects 41
Chapter 7: Turning Your Craft into a Business 51
Chapter 8: Creating Practical Macramé Items 57
Chapter 9: Beginner-Friendly DIY Projects 64
Chapter 10: Crafting Your First Piece in Simple Steps 73

GINEVRA COSTA

© Copyright 2024 by:G inevra Costa-all rights reserved.

This document is intended to provide accurate and reliable information regarding the subject matter and topic covered. The publication is sold with the idea that the publisher is not required to render accounting, officially permitted, or otherwise, qualified services. If advice is required, legal or professional, an individual practising in the profession should be ordered.

This book is protected by copyright.

In no way is it legal to reproduce, duplicate, or transmit any part of this document, whether in electronic or printed form. Recording of this publication is strictly prohibited, and any archiving of this document is not permitted except with the written permission of the publisher. All rights reserved.

The respective authors own all copyrights not held by the publisher.

The information herein is offered for informational purposes only and is universal so. The presentation of the information is without contract or warranty of any kind.

Any reference to websites is provided for convenience only and can in no way serve as an endorsement. The materials on those websites are not part of the materials in this publication and use of those websites is at your own risk.

Trademarks that are used are without consent, and publication of the trademark is without permission or endorsement from the trademark owner. All trademarks and brands within this book are for clarification purposes only and are the property of the owners themselves, not affiliated with this document.

Introduction: "Discovering the Art of Macramé – Your Journey Begins Here"

Welcome to the enchanting world of macramé, where each knot you tie is a step toward creating something **beautiful** and **unique**. As you embark on this journey, imagine yourself in a cozy workshop, the gentle rustle of cords in your hands, and the quiet satisfaction of watching your creation take shape. This is not just a craft; it's a **meditative** process that allows you to **express** your creativity while finding a sense of peace.

Macramé has a rich history, yet it remains wonderfully **accessible** to all, regardless of experience. Picture yourself transforming a simple piece of rope into a stunning wall hanging or a charming plant holder. With each knot, you'll discover how **empowering** it is to bring your ideas to life. You don't need a vast array of tools or prior knowledge—just a willingness to learn and a desire to create.

In today's fast-paced world, many of us seek activities that offer a respite from our busy lives. Macramé provides just that—a **calming** escape where you can lose yourself in the rhythm of tying knots. It's an opportunity to slow down, focus, and enjoy the simple pleasure of making something with your hands. As you progress, you'll find that macramé is not just about the finished product, but about the **joy** of the process itself.

Throughout this book, you'll receive **gentle guidance** and **supportive** advice, as if I were right there beside you. Each project is designed to build your confidence, allowing you to master fundamental skills while creating pieces that reflect your personal style. Together, we'll explore the versatility of macramé, from intricate wall art to functional home decor. So, take a deep breath, gather your materials, and let's begin this delightful journey into the art of macramé. Your path to crafting **beautiful**, **handmade** decor starts here.

Threads and beads for macramé

Chapter 1: Getting Started with Macramé

Welcome to the beginning of your **macramé journey**. Here, we'll explore the basics, ensuring you feel both **excited** and **prepared** to dive into this creative craft. Before we start knotting, let's talk about what you'll need and how to set up a comfortable workspace.

Materials are the foundation of your projects, and choosing the right ones can enhance your experience. For beginners, I recommend starting with **cotton cord**. It's easy to work with, soft to the touch, and offers a beautiful finish. Look for a thickness that feels comfortable in your hands, typically around 3-5mm, as it's forgiving and easy to manipulate.

You'll also need a pair of **sharp scissors** to ensure clean cuts, and a **measuring tape** to help you achieve the correct lengths. A **macramé board** or a simple piece of cardboard can serve as your workspace to secure your cords. Consider using **pins** to hold your work in place, especially as you're getting used to the tension and flow of knotting.

Now, let's talk about your **workspace**. Find a spot that's well-lit and comfortable. You'll be spending some time here, so make sure it's a place where you can relax and focus. A sturdy table or desk is ideal, and a comfortable chair will make your crafting sessions more enjoyable. Keep your tools within arm's reach, and perhaps play some calming music to enhance the experience.

As you prepare to start, remember that **patience** and **practice** are your best friends. Every knot you tie is a step towards creating something beautiful. Embrace the process, and don't rush. If a knot feels challenging, take a deep breath, and try again. You're here to enjoy and learn, and I'm here to guide you every step of the way.

1.1-What is Macramé?: Origins and significance of the craft

Macramé, with its intricate knots and timeless elegance, has a rich history that dates back centuries. This beloved craft, which involves creating decorative patterns by knotting cords, has been a part of various cultures, each adding its unique touch to the art form. From its origins in the Arab world, where it was known as "migramah," meaning "fringe," macramé traveled across continents, finding its way into the hands of sailors who used it to pass time during long voyages. These sailors played a crucial role in spreading macramé to different parts of the world, creating a tapestry of techniques and styles.

The craft gained prominence in Europe during the 13th century, where it was used to adorn everything from household items to clothing. The Victorians were particularly fond of macramé, using it to embellish their homes with intricate lace-like patterns. Fast forward to the 1970s, and macramé experienced a resurgence, becoming synonymous with the bohemian lifestyle. Its appeal lay in the simplicity of the materials and the meditative process of knotting, which resonated with the era's ethos of self-expression and creativity.

Today, macramé is experiencing yet another revival, beloved for its ability to blend tradition with modern aesthetics. As you embark on your own macramé journey, you are not just learning a craft; you are becoming part of a rich tapestry of history and culture. With each knot, you connect with artisans from the past, weaving your own story into the fabric of this ancient art. Embrace the journey, and let the soothing rhythm of knotting bring peace and beauty into your life.

1.2-Choosing Your Supplies: Guide to ropes, dowels, and embellishments

Welcome to the delightful world of macramé, where the right supplies can transform your creative visions into reality. Let's start with the heart of any macramé project: the **rope**. Choosing the right type of rope is essential, as it affects both the look and durability of your creations. For beginners, I recommend starting with **cotton rope**. It's soft, easy to handle, and perfect for practicing those fundamental knots. As you gain confidence, you might explore other materials like **jute** or **hemp**, each offering a unique texture and aesthetic.

Next, consider the **dowels** or supports for your projects. These are the backbone of your wall hangings and plant holders. Wooden dowels are a popular choice, providing a sturdy and natural look. Alternatively, you might experiment with **metal rods** for a modern twist or even **driftwood** for a rustic, bohemian feel. Remember, the dowel isn't just a support; it's part of the art, so choose one that complements your design.

Finally, let's talk about **embellishments**. These are the little touches that make your macramé projects uniquely yours. Beads, feathers, and even colorful threads can add personality and flair. When selecting embellishments, think about the overall style you wish to achieve. Are you aiming for a minimalist look? Perhaps stick to a few subtle beads. Want something more vibrant? Don't be afraid to mix and match different elements for a burst of creativity.

With these supplies in hand, you're well on your way to creating beautiful, personalized macramé pieces that not only decorate your home but also bring a sense of calm and accomplishment. Happy knotting!

Variety of macramé cords in different colours and textures, arranged alongside small sample projects

1.3-Setting Up Your Workspace: Creating a comfortable crafting area

Imagine a cozy corner in your home, where creativity flows as freely as the coffee in your mug. This is your **macramé sanctuary**, a space tailored to inspire and nurture your crafting journey. Start by selecting a spot with **ample natural light**, as it not only enhances your mood but also makes it easier to see detailed knots.

Consider a comfortable chair that supports your back during long crafting sessions. A **sturdy table** or desk is essential, providing a stable surface for your tools and materials. Keep your workspace **organized** with baskets or containers for cords and beads, ensuring everything is within arm's reach.

Personalize your area with elements that spark joy—perhaps a plant, a favorite quote, or a small speaker for soothing music. This is your creative haven, where each knot brings you closer to crafting **beautiful home decor** with ease and confidence.

Chapter 2: Mastering the Basics of Knots

Welcome to the heart of macramé: the art of knotting. Imagine each knot as a brushstroke in a painting, contributing to the larger masterpiece. In this chapter, we'll explore the fundamental knots that form the backbone of your macramé journey. These knots are not just techniques; they are the building blocks of your creativity.

Let's start with the **Square Knot**. This versatile knot is perhaps the most iconic in macramé. Begin by taking four cords, with the two outer cords as working cords and the two inner as filler cords. Cross the left working cord over the filler cords and under the right working cord. Then, bring the right working cord under the filler cords and through the loop created by the left working cord. Tighten to form the first half. Repeat the process in reverse to complete the knot. The beauty of the square knot lies in its symmetry and strength, making it perfect for a variety of projects.

Next, let's delve into the **Half Hitch**. This knot is the essence of simplicity and elegance. Using two cords, take the left cord over the right, then under and through the loop. Pull tight to secure. The Half Hitch is often used in series to create a spiral or diagonal pattern, adding texture and movement to your designs.

Another essential knot is the **Lark's Head Knot**. Often used to attach cords to a dowel or ring, it's both functional and decorative. Fold your cord in half, creating a loop. Place the loop over the dowel, bring the ends through the loop, and pull tight. This knot is your starting point for many macramé pieces, anchoring your design and setting the stage for creativity.

Finally, the **Double Half Hitch** is a combination of two Half Hitches, creating a secure and decorative line. Begin with a Half Hitch, then repeat the process with the same cords. This knot is ideal for creating horizontal or diagonal patterns, adding structure and detail to your work.

With these knots in your repertoire, you're well-equipped to embark on your macramé journey. Remember, each knot is a step towards crafting something beautiful and uniquely yours. Embrace the process, and enjoy the rhythm of knotting as you bring your creative visions to life.

Josephine knot

2.1-Introduction to Simple Knots: Essential beginner knots explained

Welcome to the world of macramé, where each knot is a step towards creating something **beautiful and personalized** for your home. As you begin this journey, you'll discover how simple knots can transform into stunning pieces of decor. Let's dive into the basics, starting with the most essential knots every beginner should master.

The first knot we'll explore is the **Square Knot**. This knot is the foundation for many macramé projects. Begin by taking two cords, holding them parallel. Cross the left cord over the center cords, then bring it under the right cord. Now, take the right cord, pass it under the center cords, and through the loop created by the left cord. Pull both ends to tighten. Practice this a few times, and you'll see how it forms a neat, flat knot.

Next, let's try the **Half Hitch Knot**. This knot is perfect for creating diagonal patterns. Start by holding the working cord in your left hand, and the filler cord in your right. Wrap the working cord over and around the filler cord, pulling it through the loop. Tighten the knot by pulling the working cord upwards. Repeat this process to create a series of half hitches, forming a lovely, textured line.

Finally, the **Lark's Head Knot** is often used to attach cords to a dowel or ring. Fold your cord in half to create a loop. Place the loop over the dowel, then bring the ends through the loop and pull tight. This knot is simple yet effective, providing a secure starting point for many designs.

Remember, each knot you learn is a building block towards creating your own unique macramé pieces. As you practice, you'll find a rhythm that is both **calming and rewarding**. Embrace the process, and let your creativity flow with every twist and pull.

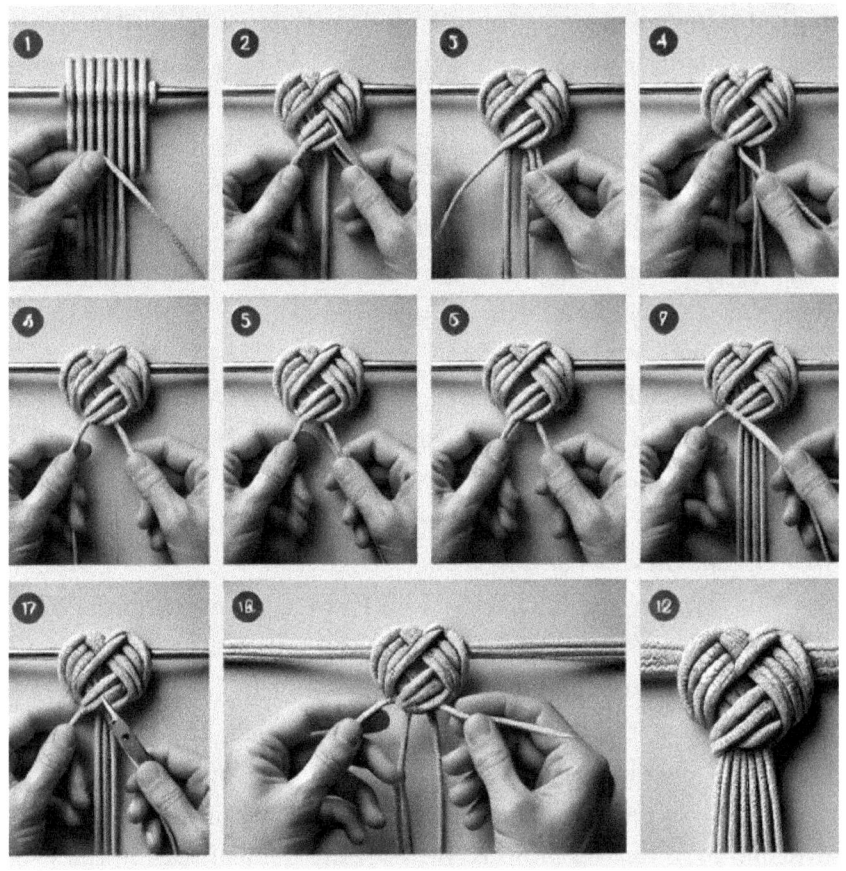

Here is a picture illustrating the step-by-step process to create a " Square knot" in macramé, designed to clearly guide beginners through each step.

2.2-Building on Basics: Intermediate knotting techniques

As we journey into the realm of intermediate macramé, it's time to expand your knotting repertoire. With these techniques, you'll be able to create more intricate and stunning designs, adding a touch of elegance and complexity to your projects.

Let's begin with the **Square Knot** variations. You've mastered the basic square knot, but did you know that by alternating them, you can create a beautiful, textured pattern known as the **Josephine Knot**? This knot is perfect for adding a decorative flair to your wall hangings. Simply start with a square knot, then alternate the cords to tie another square knot, creating a lovely twist effect.

Next, the **Half Hitch** can be transformed into a **Double Half Hitch**, which is essential for creating diagonal lines and curves in your designs. To achieve this, tie a half hitch, then follow it with another half hitch using the same cord. This technique is fantastic for crafting intricate patterns like chevrons or waves.

Now, let's explore the **Lark's Head Knot** in its reverse form. While the standard lark's head is great for attaching cords to a dowel, the reverse version adds texture and dimension. Instead of looping the cord over the dowel, loop it under, then pull the ends through. This subtle change creates a distinct look, perfect for adding variety to your macramé pieces.

Finally, the **Spiral Knot**, a variation of the half knot, can add a dynamic twist to your projects. By repeating the half knot in the same direction, you'll create a spiraling effect, ideal for plant hangers or decorative fringes.

With these intermediate techniques, you're well on your way to creating macramé masterpieces that not only enhance your home decor but also bring you joy and relaxation in the crafting process.

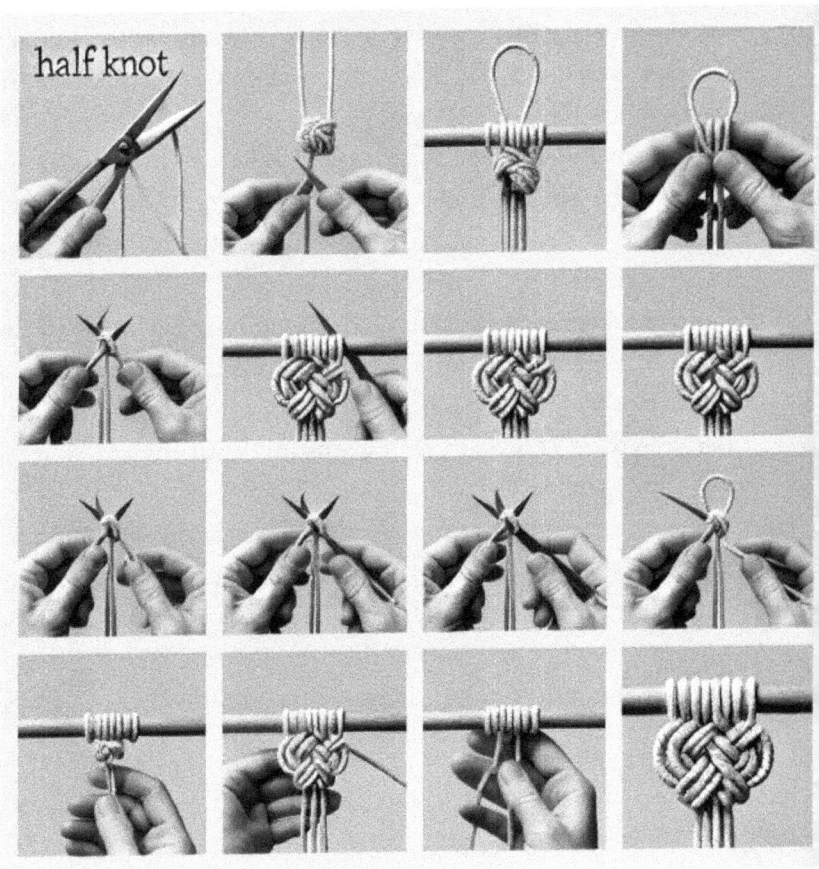

2.3-Creative Knotting Patterns: Combining knots for unique textures

As you embark on your journey into creative knotting, remember that each knot is like a word in a language, and together they can tell a beautiful story through texture and form. Let's explore how combining knots can lead to unique and stunning patterns that can elevate your macramé projects.

Begin with the **Square Knot**, a fundamental building block in macramé. By alternating rows of square knots, you can create a

checkerboard effect, adding a playful texture to your design. Don't hesitate to experiment with the **spacing** between knots to achieve different levels of density and openness.

Another versatile knot is the **Half Hitch**. When used in succession, it forms the **Spiral Stitch**, a dynamic pattern that adds movement and flow. This is perfect for creating elements that draw the eye, such as twisting plant hangers or decorative fringes.

For a more intricate texture, try combining **Lark's Head Knots** with **Double Half Hitch Knots**. This combination can result in a **diamond pattern**, which adds a geometric elegance to your work. The interplay between these knots can create a sense of depth, making your piece more visually engaging.

As you practice, let your creativity guide you. Mix and match these knots, play with their arrangements, and watch as your confidence grows with each creation. Remember, the beauty of macramé lies not just in the final product, but in the **joy of the process** itself. Embrace the meditative rhythm of knotting and let it inspire your unique artistic expression.

The image shows the "**Square Knot**" (or "**Reef Knot**"), one of the most fundamental knots in macramé.

Here's a breakdown of its features and technique:

1. "Structure": The Square Knot is made using four strands: two outer strands that are used to create the knot, and two inner strands that stay in the center as the knot is formed.

2. "Technique":
- Start by bringing the left outer strand over the two center strands and under the right outer strand.
- Then, bring the right outer strand under the two center strands and over the left strand.
- Tighten both sides to complete the first half of the knot.
- Repeat the steps, reversing sides to create a balanced, square shape.

This knot is widely used in macramé projects due to its simplicity and versatility, creating a strong and visually appealing pattern suitable for wall hangings, plant hangers, and more.

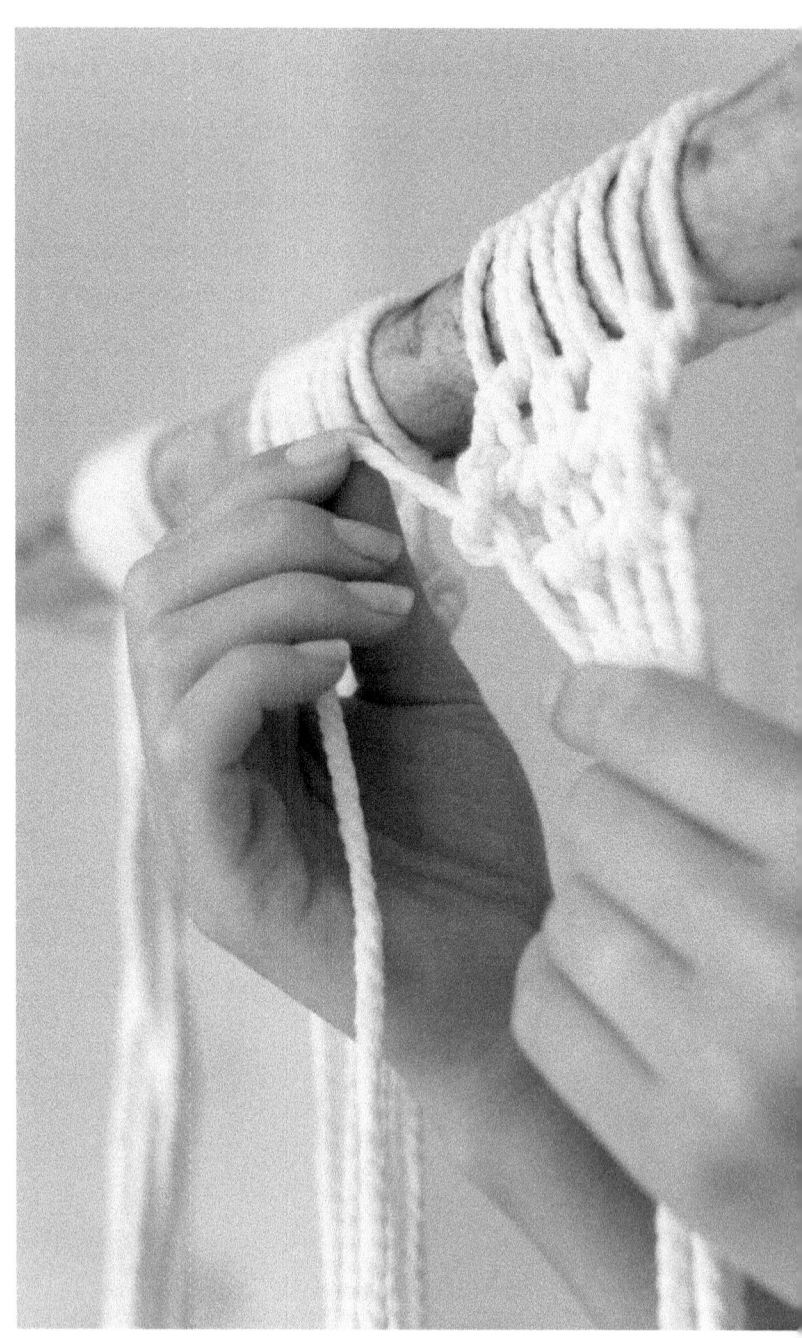

Chapter 3: Exploring Macramé Styles

As we delve into the world of macramé, you'll soon discover that this art form is as diverse as it is beautiful. Each style offers a unique perspective, allowing your creativity to flourish in unexpected ways. Imagine sitting in a sunlit room, a gentle breeze playing with the strands of rope as you embark on your next project. This is where the magic of macramé truly begins to unfold.

One of the most enchanting aspects of macramé is its **versatility**. From the intricate patterns of **bohemian** designs to the clean lines of **modern minimalism**, macramé can transform any space with its charm. As you explore these styles, consider what resonates with your personal aesthetic. Perhaps you are drawn to the **earthy textures** of natural fibers, or maybe the **bold colors** of contemporary pieces speak to your artistic soul. Whatever your preference, there's a style waiting to be discovered.

Picture a cozy corner of your home adorned with a **vintage-inspired wall hanging**. The knots tell a story of tradition, echoing the craftsmanship of artisans from decades past. This style, rich with history, brings a sense of nostalgia, yet it feels perfectly at home in today's world. On the other hand, envision a sleek, modern macramé plant holder, its simplicity highlighting the beauty of the plant it cradles. Such pieces are perfect for those who appreciate the elegance of minimalism.

As you create, remember that macramé is more than just a decorative art—it's a journey of **self-expression**. Each knot you tie is a step towards crafting something uniquely yours. Don't be afraid to experiment with **different materials** and **colors**. The beauty of macramé lies in its ability to evolve with you, adapting to your changing tastes and inspirations.

In this chapter, I encourage you to explore these styles with an open heart and a curious mind. Let the strands of macramé guide you to new discoveries, and embrace the **calming rhythm** of knotting as a form of meditation. With each project, you'll gain confidence and insight, creating pieces that not only adorn your home but also reflect your journey as a budding macramé artist.

3.1-Popular Design Themes: From bohemian to minimalist

As you embark on your macramé journey, you'll find that the art of knotting can beautifully complement a variety of design themes. Whether your heart leans towards the free-spirited vibes of bohemian decor or the clean lines of minimalism, macramé offers a versatile touch that can enhance any space.

Let's explore the bohemian style first. Known for its eclectic mix of textures and colors, bohemian decor embraces the natural, earthy elements that macramé embodies. Imagine a vibrant wall hanging with intricate patterns, adding a splash of creativity to your living room. The beauty of bohemian macramé lies in its freedom and spontaneity. You can mix different types of knots and incorporate beads or feathers to create pieces that are uniquely yours.

On the other end of the spectrum, we find the minimalist approach. Here, the focus is on simplicity and functionality. Macramé can contribute to a minimalist space by offering subtle elegance. Think of a sleek, monochrome plant hanger that adds a touch of nature without overwhelming the room. The key to minimalist macramé is to keep the designs clean and understated, using fewer knots and focusing on high-quality materials.

Regardless of your preferred style, macramé allows you to express your personality and bring a sense of calm and creativity into your home. Remember, each knot is a step towards crafting a space that feels truly yours. Enjoy the process, and let your imagination guide you in blending these themes to create a harmonious environment.

3.2-Popular Design Themes: From bohemian to minimalist

As you embark on your macramé journey, you'll discover that the art of knotting can be beautifully versatile, adapting to various design themes that can reflect your personal style and the ambiance you wish to create in your home. One popular theme is the **bohemian style**, known for its eclectic and free-spirited vibe. This style embraces a mix of textures, colors, and patterns, often featuring intricate macramé pieces that add a touch of whimsy and warmth. Imagine a macramé wall hanging with flowing fringes, bringing a sense of wanderlust and creativity to your living space.

On the other end of the spectrum, the **minimalist design** celebrates simplicity and functionality. Here, macramé pieces are often characterized by clean lines and neutral tones, offering a subtle yet elegant touch to any room. A minimalist macramé plant holder, for instance, can add a breath of fresh air without overwhelming the space, perfectly complementing a serene and uncluttered environment.

Whether you lean towards the bohemian or minimalist aesthetic, or perhaps find yourself somewhere in between, macramé offers endless possibilities to express your unique taste. As you create, consider the **mood and atmosphere** you wish to evoke. Each knot and pattern can contribute to a sense of harmony and balance, enhancing the overall feel of your home. Remember, the beauty of macramé lies in its ability to adapt and transform, much like the creative journey you are about to undertake.

Popular macramé design themes, from intricate bohemian styles with knots and layered fringes to clean, minimalist designs.

Large round tapestry (top left):

This circular piece is made with a concentric knot technique that creates a mandala-like pattern. Starting from the centre, the rings of knots expand outwards evenly, with a structure that appears well-calibrated and detailed. At the end of the circle, there are long, dense fringes that hang symmetrically downwards, adding an effect of lightness to the piece.

Image 2: Large tapestry with fringes and decorative circles: This tapestry has a triangular structure and features a symmetrical, mandala-like motif in the centre, which adds depth to the composition. Two decorative circles, positioned to the upper left and right of the central motif, enrich the design and bring balance. The lower part has long fringes that extend neatly downwards, emphasising the verticality of the piece and creating a relaxing visual effect. The colour palette remains neutral, with cream and beige tones that suit a minimalist or bohemian ambience.

Image3: Square tapestry with tassels and geometric motifs: This piece has a square structure and a series of tassels hanging at the bottom, giving movement and a touch of elegance. The upper part of the tapestry is decorated with a network of geometric knots, creating an almost three-dimensional effect. The symmetrical arrangement of the knots and tassels makes this tapestry particularly suitable as a central piece in a wall composition.

Image 4:Tapestry with fan and fringe detail:** In this image, the tapestry is structured with a fan motif that opens towards the base, decorated with fringes that descend in an orderly fashion. The central motif is formed by a series of knots that create a semicircle design, emphasised by the long fringes that thin out at the bottom. Its open shape is reminiscent of a feather or flower, giving a sense of naturalness and lightness.

3.3-Adapting Styles to Projects: Matching

patterns to your space

When it comes to crafting macramé pieces, the beauty lies in how they seamlessly blend into your living space, adding a touch of **personalized elegance**. The key to achieving this harmony is to adapt styles to suit your unique environment. Let's explore how you can match macramé patterns to your home decor.

First, consider the **overall aesthetic** of your space. Is your home more modern, bohemian, or perhaps a mix of both? For a minimalist setting, opt for patterns that are **clean and simple**, using neutral tones that complement the existing color palette. A simple wall hanging with a few intricate knots can add just the right amount of texture without overwhelming the room.

If your decor leans towards a bohemian style, embrace the **rich textures** and **earthy colors** that macramé naturally offers. Experiment with **layered patterns** and vibrant hues. A large, colorful macramé piece can become a focal point, infusing the space with warmth and creativity.

Next, think about the **functionality** of the space. In a living room, a macramé wall hanging can serve as a stunning backdrop, while in a kitchen, a macramé plant holder might be the perfect way to bring in a touch of nature. Each piece should not only enhance the visual appeal but also contribute to the **ambiance** and **purpose** of the room.

Finally, remember that macramé is about **expression**. Use it to tell your story. Whether you're creating a piece for a cozy corner or a vibrant living area, let your personal style shine through. The beauty of macramé is its ability to be both an art form and a reflection of your unique taste.

By thoughtfully adapting styles to your projects, you'll create macramé pieces that not only decorate but also resonate with the heart of your home.

3.4-Color and Texture Choices: Adding

character to your pieces

When embarking on your macramé journey, the choices of **color and texture** are like the brushstrokes of a painter, each decision adding unique character and charm to your creations. Imagine your home as a blank canvas, waiting to be adorned with the warmth of handcrafted art.

Start by considering the **ambiance** you wish to create. Do you desire a **calming, neutral palette** that whispers serenity, or are you drawn to **vibrant hues** that spark joy and energy? Your color choices can dramatically influence the mood of a room. Soft, earthy tones can evoke a sense of tranquility, while bold, contrasting colors can energize and enliven a space.

Texture plays an equally vital role. The feel of the cord beneath your fingers can transform your crafting experience. A **smooth, silky cord** might lend a modern, sleek finish, while a **rougher, natural fiber** can bring a rustic, organic touch. Consider mixing different textures to add depth and interest to your work, creating a tactile feast for the senses.

Remember, macramé is a journey of **self-expression**. Let your instincts guide you in selecting colors and textures that reflect your personal style and the atmosphere you wish to cultivate. Each knot you tie is a step towards a more personalized, inviting home.

Chapter 4: Helpful Techniques and Shortcuts

As you delve deeper into the world of macramé, it's natural to seek out those little **tricks** and **shortcuts** that can make your crafting experience both easier and more enjoyable. Imagine yourself sitting in a cozy nook, surrounded by the soft glow of afternoon light, your favorite music playing gently in the background. This is your time, and with a few helpful techniques, your macramé journey can become even more fulfilling.

Let's start with the **importance of tension**. Think of it as the heartbeat of your project. Consistent tension ensures that your knots are uniform, creating a polished look. Picture the threads as dancers, each step measured and graceful, moving in harmony to create a beautiful performance. Practice this by gently pulling each knot with equal pressure, letting your fingers develop a rhythm that feels right.

Now, consider the **magic of pre-cutting** your cords. By preparing your materials in advance, you free your mind to focus on the creative flow rather than stopping to measure. Lay out your cords, envisioning the final piece, and let the anticipation of crafting build as you cut each length with precision.

Another delightful technique is to use **markers** or **clips** to keep your place. These little aids act like bookmarks in a favorite novel, allowing you to pause and return without losing the thread of your story. They offer a gentle reminder of where you left off, so you can continue your creative journey without interruption.

Finally, embrace the **joy of experimentation**. As you become more comfortable with the basics, allow yourself to play with different textures and colors. Imagine your macramé as a canvas, each knot a brushstroke that adds depth and vibrancy to your creation. Trust your instincts and let your imagination guide you to new and exciting designs.

Incorporating these techniques into your crafting routine will not only enhance your skills but also deepen your connection to the art of macramé. Remember, every knot is a step forward, a moment of mindfulness that brings you closer to creating something truly beautiful.

4.1-Achieving Consistent Tension: Tips for smooth, even knots

As you embark on your macramé journey, achieving **consistent tension** in your knots is essential. This ensures that your projects have a **smooth and professional appearance**. Think of tension as the gentle pressure you apply while knotting, akin to tuning a musical instrument. Too tight, and the strings might snap; too loose, and the melody falters. Here, we'll explore some simple yet effective tips to help you master this crucial skill.

First, **set the stage** for your macramé work. Choose a comfortable, well-lit space where you can easily see your cords. This will help you maintain focus and consistency. Before you begin knotting, take a moment to **relax your hands** and shoulders. Tension in your body can translate to tension in your knots, so a calm, steady posture is your best ally.

As you start knotting, pay attention to your **grip on the cords**. Hold them firmly, but not too tightly. Imagine holding a delicate bird in your hand—enough to keep it safe, but not enough to cause discomfort. This gentle grip allows you to control the tension without straining your fingers.

Another key aspect is **consistency in your movements**. As you pull each knot tight, try to use the same amount of force each time. This might take a little practice, but with each knot, you'll develop a rhythm. If you notice a knot that looks out of place, don't hesitate to undo it and try again. Remember, macramé is as much about the process as the final product.

Lastly, take breaks when needed. Knotting can be meditative, but it's important to listen to your body. A short pause can refresh your mind and help maintain that **even tension** throughout your work. With patience and practice, you'll find your own rhythm, and your projects will reflect the beauty of your consistent effort.

4.2-Troubleshooting Common Issues: Fixing mistakes and loose ends

As you embark on your macramé journey, it's natural to encounter a few **bumps** along the way. But fear not! With a little patience and practice, you'll be able to turn those knots into a beautiful tapestry of success. Let's explore some common issues and how to address them.

Uneven Tension

If you notice that some of your knots are tighter or looser than others, don't worry—this is a common occurrence for beginners. The key is to **maintain consistent tension** as you work. Try to pull each knot with the same amount of force. It might help to practice on a scrap piece of cord until you feel comfortable.

Twisted Cords

Twisting can make your project look less polished. To fix this, ensure that your cords are **straightened and untangled** before starting. If they become twisted during the process, gently untwist them before proceeding with the next knot.

Incorrect Knots

We all make mistakes, and it's okay to undo a knot if it doesn't look right. Carefully **reverse the knot** by retracing your steps, then try again. Remember, practice makes perfect, and each mistake is an opportunity to learn.

Loose Ends

Loose ends can detract from the neatness of your piece. To secure them, consider using a dab of fabric glue or tying a small knot at the end of each cord. This will help keep everything in place and give your project a more polished look.

By addressing these common issues, you'll gain confidence and enjoy the meditative process of macramé even more. Remember, each project is a step forward in your crafting journey, and every knot brings you closer to creating something truly special.

4.3-Finishing Touches and Care: Ensuring durability and quality

As you complete your macramé masterpiece, it's time to focus on those **finishing touches** that ensure both durability and quality. These final steps are crucial in transforming your creation from a simple craft project into a cherished piece of art.

First, let's talk about **securing your knots**. A well-secured knot is the backbone of any macramé piece. Gently tug on each knot to confirm it's tight and holds its place. If needed, add a drop of fabric glue to the back of complex knots to maintain their shape over time.

Next, consider the **trimming and tidying** of excess cord. Use sharp scissors to cut cords evenly, ensuring a clean finish. If you prefer a fringed look, take the time to **comb through the ends** with a fine-tooth comb, allowing the fibers to separate and create a soft, flowing effect.

For pieces like plant hangers or wall hangings, **consider the weight** they will bear. Reinforce areas that will experience tension by doubling up on knots or using thicker cords. This will enhance the strength and longevity of your creation.

Finally, caring for your macramé involves **gentle cleaning**. Dust your pieces regularly with a soft brush. If deeper cleaning is required, hand wash with mild soap and cold water, then lay flat to dry, reshaping as needed to maintain its form.

By attending to these details, you ensure that your macramé project not only looks beautiful but also stands the test of time, ready to be admired for years to come.

Chapter 5: Macramé for Relaxation and Mindfulness

As you settle into the gentle rhythm of macramé, you might find yourself naturally drawn to its calming effects. This isn't merely a happy coincidence; it's one of the craft's most cherished benefits. In our fast-paced world, finding moments of **peace and tranquility** can be challenging. Yet, with macramé, each knot becomes a meditative act, a chance to focus solely on the **present moment.**

Imagine sitting with your materials, the soft texture of the cord slipping through your fingers, the quiet rustle as you pull each knot tight. This tactile experience is not just about creating something beautiful; it's about **connecting with yourself** and the world around you. As you learn to trust your hands to guide the knots, you also learn to trust in the process of **letting go** of stress and embracing the simplicity of creation.

Macramé offers a unique opportunity to cultivate **mindfulness**. Each project, whether it's a simple keychain or an elaborate wall hanging, encourages you to focus on the task at hand. There's a certain magic in watching your work unfold, each knot building upon the last, forming patterns that are both intricate and serene. This focus helps quiet the mind, allowing worries to fade into the background.

In these moments, you might discover a newfound appreciation for the **art of patience**. Macramé teaches us that beauty takes time and effort, and that each step, however small, is a vital part of the whole. Embrace the journey, knowing that every knot tied is a step toward **inner peace** and fulfillment. As you weave, remember that this is your time—a gift to yourself, a chance to unwind and reconnect with the simple joys of life.

Image of macramé supplies

Including cords, wooden dowels, beads, and rings, neatly arranged for easy viewing of each material's details and texture.

5.1-Crafting as Therapy: Using macramé to de-stress

As you settle into the rhythmic flow of knotting, you'll find that macramé offers more than just the creation of beautiful decor. It becomes a **sanctuary of calm** amid the hustle and bustle of daily life. Each knot you tie is a step away from stress and toward a place of inner peace.

Imagine this: a quiet corner, soft music playing in the background, and the feel of the cord slipping through your fingers. This is your time, a moment to **unplug** and focus solely on the task at hand. The repetitive nature of macramé is akin to meditation, where the act of creating becomes a **gentle mantra**, soothing your mind and easing tension.

In our fast-paced world, it's easy to feel overwhelmed. That's where macramé steps in, offering a **tangible escape**. As you work on your projects, you'll notice your breathing slows, your thoughts become clearer, and a sense of accomplishment begins to build. It's not just about the finished piece; it's about the journey you take to get there.

While crafting, you may find yourself entering a state of **flow**, where time seems to slip away, and you are fully immersed in the present. This state is incredibly beneficial, reducing anxiety and promoting a sense of well-being. Macramé invites you to embrace this flow, allowing your creativity to flourish without the pressure of perfection.

Remember, each knot is a step toward **mindfulness**. Allow yourself to savor the process, to feel the texture of the materials, and to appreciate the beauty of simplicity. In this space, stress fades, and you are left with a profound sense of **calm** and satisfaction. Let macramé be your guide to relaxation, one knot at a time.

Macramé for Relaxation and Mindfulness

5.2-Creating a Calming Practice: Building a mindful macramé routine

As you embark on your macramé journey, it's essential to recognize the **transformative power** of crafting as a mindful practice. Macramé offers a unique opportunity to **immerse yourself** in the present moment, allowing the repetitive motions of knotting to become a form of meditation.

Begin by setting aside a **dedicated space** for your macramé work. Whether it's a cozy corner in your living room or a spot by the window, ensure this space is free from distractions. Surround yourself with items that inspire tranquility, perhaps a potted plant or a softly scented candle.

Before you start knotting, take a moment to **center yourself**. Close your eyes, take a few deep breaths, and let go of any tension. This simple act of mindfulness prepares your mind and body for the calming rhythm of macramé.

As you work, focus on the **texture** of the cord, the way it feels between your fingers, and the gentle pull as you tighten each knot. Allow yourself to **revel in the simplicity** of the process, appreciating the beauty of each completed section. Remember, there is no rush; the journey is just as important as the finished piece.

Consider incorporating a **ritual** into your crafting routine. Perhaps you start each session with a cup of tea or play your favorite soothing music. These small rituals can enhance the meditative quality of your practice, making each macramé session a cherished part of your day.

Embrace any mistakes as part of the learning process. Each knot is a step towards **mastery**, and each project is a testament to your growth. With patience and practice, you'll find that macramé not only enriches your home but also nurtures your spirit.

The image shows the Lark's Head Knot;

one of the most basic and essential knots in macramé.

Characteristics:

Type: Attaching knot, often used to secure cords to a dowel, branch, or ring.

Structure: Created by folding the cord in half, then looping it around the dowel and pulling the ends through the loop, which secures the cord to the base.

Technique:
Fold the cord in half to create a loop.
Place the loop over the dowel (or other base material).
Pull the two ends of the cord through the loop.
Tighten by pulling down on the ends until secure.

The Lark's Head Knot is widely used as the starting knot in many macramé projects, providing a stable and visually clean way to attach cords. It's commonly seen in wall hangings, plant hangers, and decorative pieces.

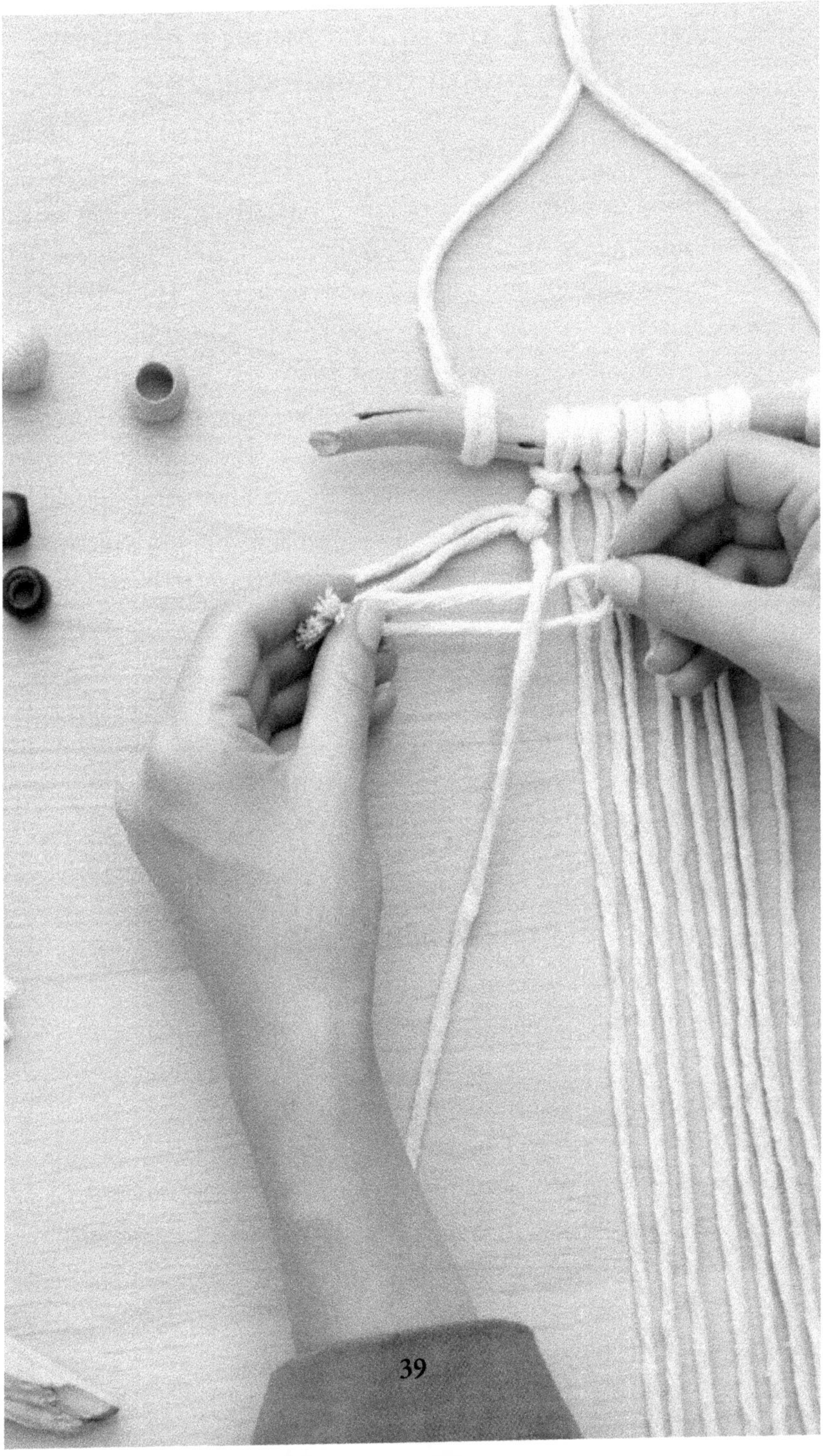

5.3 - Focus and Flow in Macramé: Enhancing concentration through crafting

Imagine sitting in a cozy corner of your home, the gentle light of the afternoon sun spilling across your workspace. In front of you, a simple piece of cord transforms into a delicate pattern, knot by knot. This is the magic of macramé—a craft that not only results in beautiful decor but also offers a profound sense of **focus and flow**.

As you begin to work with macramé, you'll find that it requires just the right amount of **attention and precision**. The repetitive motions of knotting can be incredibly soothing, almost meditative. Each knot becomes a rhythm, a beat in the symphony of your crafting journey. This rhythmic action helps to **quiet the mind**, allowing you to focus solely on the task at hand.

In our fast-paced world, finding moments of tranquility can be challenging. Macramé offers a unique opportunity to **slow down** and immerse yourself in a creative process that is both calming and rewarding. As you engage with the cords, you may notice a shift in your mindset. The concerns of daily life begin to fade, replaced by a sense of **peace and clarity**.

Moreover, crafting with macramé encourages a **state of flow**, a concept often described as being "in the zone." This state is characterized by complete absorption in an activity, where time seems to fly by, and your skills are perfectly matched to the challenge. Achieving this flow state through macramé not only enhances your concentration but also leaves you with a sense of fulfillment and accomplishment.

So, as you embark on your macramé projects, embrace the process. Allow yourself to be present with each knot, each twist of the cord. Let the craft guide you to a place of **focus and serenity**, where creativity flourishes and the world outside gently fades away.

Chapter 6: Inspiring Macramé Projects

As the sun sets, casting a warm glow over your living space, imagine the serene beauty of a macramé wall hanging catching the last light of the day. In this chapter, we'll explore how to create such **inspiring pieces**, bringing both beauty and tranquility into your home. Picture yourself unwinding after a long day, the rhythmic knotting of macramé offering a meditative escape. This is not just about crafting; it's about **creating a sanctuary** within your own walls.

Let's begin with a project that combines simplicity with elegance: the **Classic Chevron Wall Hanging**. As you start, envision the chevron pattern forming under your fingers, each knot a step toward a masterpiece. The gentle repetition of the square knot becomes a soothing mantra, guiding you through the process. Remember, each knot is a building block, a testament to your growing skills and creativity.

Next, consider the **Bohemian Plant Hanger**, a perfect blend of function and style. Picture your favorite plant cradled in a nest of soft cotton cords, suspended in the air. As you weave, imagine the lush greenery contrasting with the natural tones of the macramé, a reminder of the beauty in simplicity. This project not only enhances your space but also nurtures your connection to nature.

Finally, let's delve into the **Textured Table Runner**, a piece that adds a touch of handmade charm to any dining experience. Visualize the intricate knots forming a tapestry of texture, each one a testament to your patience and dedication. As you complete this project, you'll find a sense of accomplishment, knowing that you've created something truly unique.

Through these projects, you'll discover that macramé is more than just a craft; it's a journey toward **mindfulness and creativity**. Embrace each knot, each moment, and let your home become a canvas for your newfound skills and artistic expression.

42

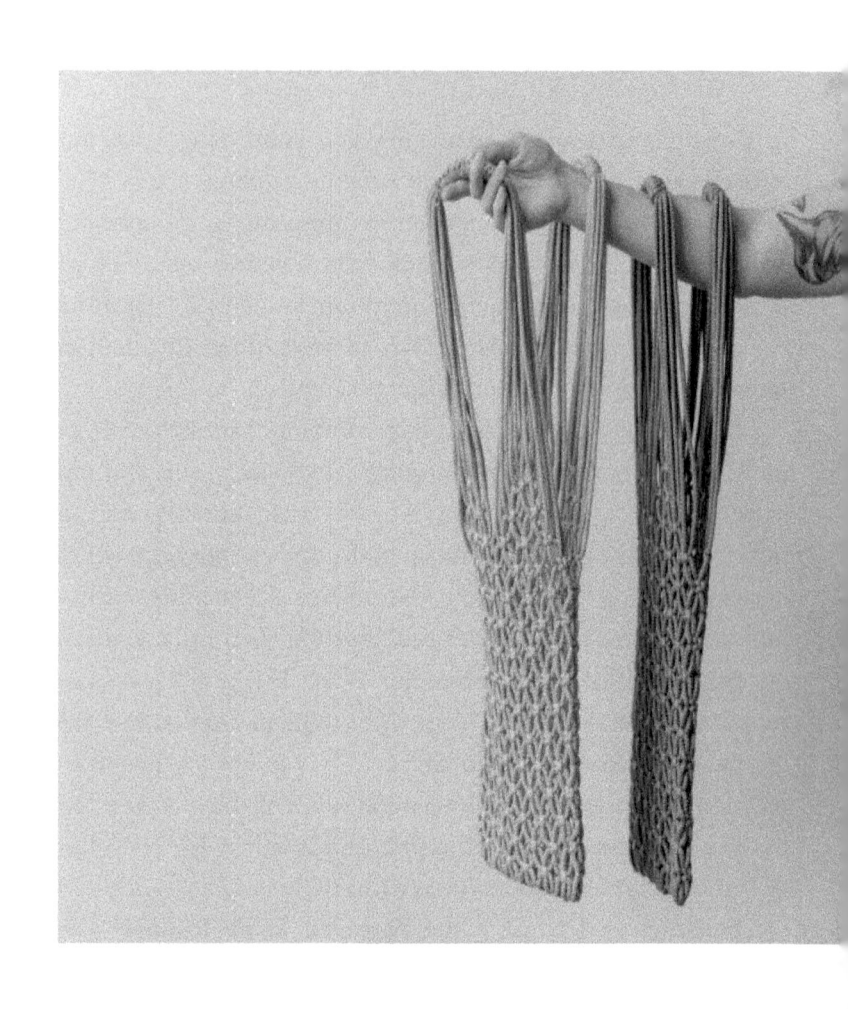

6.1-Decorative Wall Art: Bringing texture and art to any wall

Imagine a blank wall in your home, waiting to be transformed into a canvas of creativity and warmth. With macramé, you can bring **texture** and **art** to your spaces, weaving a story of intricate knots and harmonious designs. Let's explore how you can create stunning decorative wall art that not only enhances your decor but also offers a touch of handmade elegance.

Begin by selecting the right materials. Choose a **soft, durable cord** that complements your room's color palette. Cotton is a popular choice for its versatility and ease of handling. You'll also need a sturdy dowel or branch to hang your masterpiece, adding a natural element to your creation.

Start with the **basic knots** you've learned: the square knot, the half hitch, and the lark's head. These foundational techniques are your toolkit for crafting patterns that are both simple and striking. As you work, remember that macramé is as much about the **process** as the result. Allow yourself to get lost in the rhythmic repetition of knotting, finding a sense of calm with each loop and pull.

Consider incorporating **layers and dimensions** into your design. By varying the lengths of your cords and the placement of knots, you can create a piece that has depth and movement. Experiment with fringe, tassels, and beads for added flair, letting your creativity guide you.

Once your wall art is complete, step back and admire the **unique texture** it brings to your space. Each knot is a testament to your patience and creativity, a personal touch that breathes life into your home. As you hang your macramé art, feel the satisfaction of having crafted something beautiful with your own hands, a reflection of your journey into the world of macramé.

Remember, the beauty of macramé lies not just in the finished piece, but in the **joy** of crafting it. Let your wall art be a reminder of the tranquility and fulfillment that comes with creating something truly your own.

The image shows the Half Hitch Knot;

a commonly used knot in macramé that forms the basis for several decorative patterns.

Characteristics:

1. **Type**: Wrapping or binding knot, often used to create twists and patterns.
2. **Structure**: Created by looping one cord around a central cord or filler cord, then tightening to form a knot.
3. **Technique**:
    - Take the working cord and create a loop over or under the filler cord (the central strand).
    - Pass the end of the working cord through this loop.
    - Pull it tight to form a single hitch.
    - For a double half hitch, repeat the process on the same side.

This knot can be repeated in a sequence to create diagonal or horizontal patterns, commonly known as **Diagonal Half Hitch** or **Double Half Hitch Knots**. It's versatile and can be used to make spirals, waves, and detailed designs in macramé pieces.

6.2-Plant Holder Designs: Greenery displays for any space

Imagine a serene corner of your home, where a cascade of lush greenery brings life and tranquility to the space. A macramé plant holder is not just a vessel for your beloved plants; it's a piece of art that you've crafted with your own hands. Let's embark on this creative journey together, and I'll guide you through the steps to create your very own plant holder, perfect for any nook or cranny.

To start, gather your materials. You'll need some **sturdy macramé cord**, a **metal or wooden ring** for the base, and a **pair of scissors**. As you prepare your space, take a moment to envision the finished piece, its gentle sway in the breeze, and the sense of accomplishment you'll feel once it's complete.

Begin by cutting your cord into **equal lengths**. For a standard plant holder, you'll need about eight cords, each approximately four times the length you want your holder to hang. Fold each cord in half, and attach them to your ring using a simple **lark's head knot**. This knot is not only functional but also adds a touch of elegance to your design.

With your cords securely attached, it's time to create the body of the holder. We'll use a series of **square knots**, a foundational knot in macramé that offers both strength and beauty. As you work, let the rhythm of the knots guide you, finding a meditative flow in the repetition. Remember, each knot is a step closer to your vision.

Once the body is complete, gather the cords at the bottom and tie a **gathering knot** to secure your plant in place. As you tie this final knot, take a moment to admire your creation. You've transformed simple materials into a stunning display for your greenery.

Hang your plant holder in a spot where it can catch the light, and enjoy the beauty and serenity it brings to your home. With each glance, you'll be reminded of the joy of crafting and the calming power of macramé.

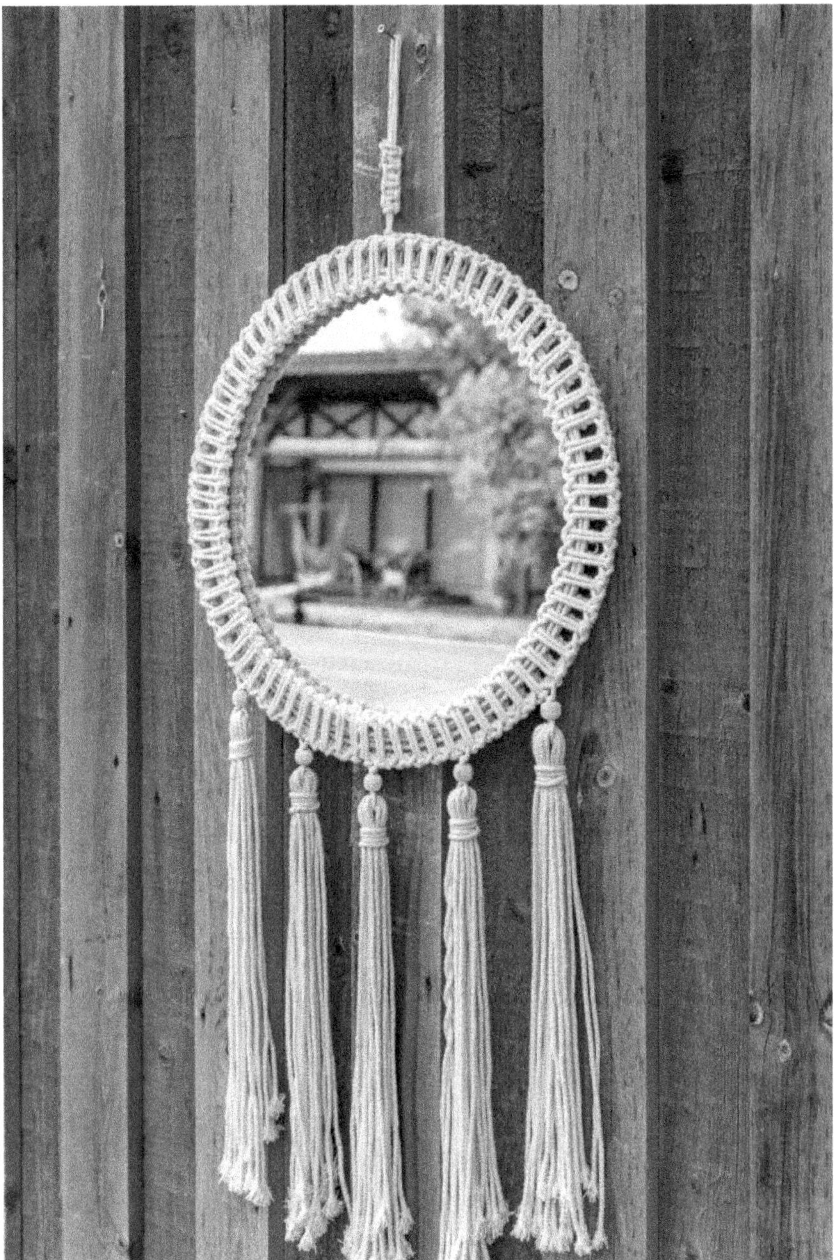

6.3-Crafting Wearables: Unique accessories like necklaces and bracelets

Welcome to the world of wearable macramé! Creating your own **necklaces and bracelets** not only offers a personal touch to your style but also lets you carry the calming essence of macramé with you wherever you go. As we dive into this chapter, remember that the beauty of macramé lies in its simplicity and the joy it brings through the process.

Let's start with a **simple bracelet**. Choose a soft, durable cord—cotton or hemp works beautifully. Cut three pieces, each about 30 inches long. Fold them in half, making a loop at the top. Secure the loop with a knot, leaving enough space to fit a small bead if you wish. This loop will serve as your clasp.

Now, anchor your work on a stable surface. Begin with the basic square knot, alternating sides to create a flat, even pattern. As you work, pause and admire the texture forming beneath your fingers. Feel free to add beads between knots for a splash of color and personality.

Once your bracelet reaches the desired length, tie off the ends with a secure knot. Trim any excess cord, leaving a small tail to prevent unraveling. Now, slip the loop over the knot to fasten your bracelet. Admire your creation—a simple yet elegant piece that speaks to your creativity.

For a **necklace**, the process is similar but offers room for more elaborate designs. Start with longer cords, around 60 inches, and consider using a mix of knots, such as the lark's head or spiral knot, to add dimension. Incorporate larger beads or pendants to serve as focal points, turning your necklace into a statement piece.

As you craft, let the rhythm of knotting bring you peace. Each twist and turn is a reminder of the meditative nature of macramé. Wear your creations with pride, knowing they are as unique as the hands that made them. Enjoy the journey, and remember, each knot is a step towards mastering this beautiful art form.

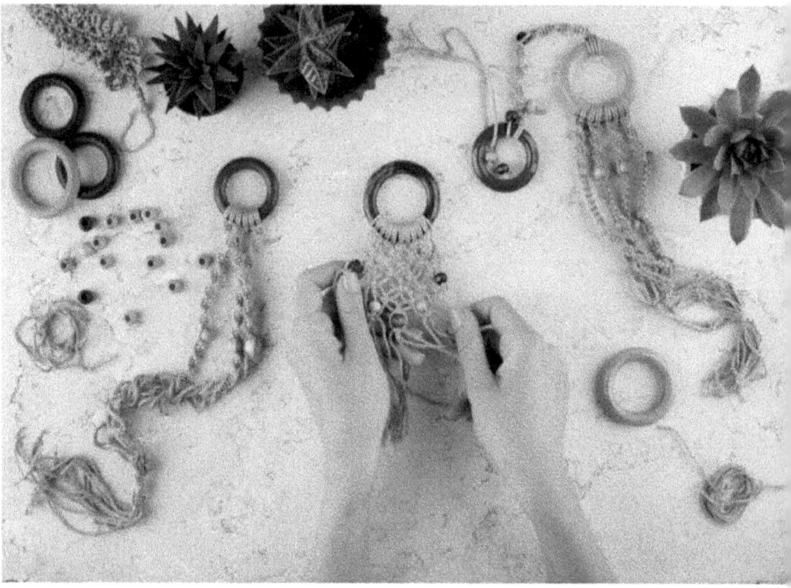

Chapter 7: Turning Your Craft into a Business

Imagine sitting in your cozy crafting nook, surrounded by spools of colorful cord and the gentle hum of creativity. As you tie each knot, you begin to wonder: could this calming hobby become a source of income? The answer is a resounding **yes**. Transitioning from crafting for pleasure to crafting for profit is a journey many have embarked on, and it all begins with passion and a dash of entrepreneurial spirit.

Start by envisioning your **unique style**. What sets your macramé apart? It might be the intricate designs or the natural materials you use. Identifying your niche is the first step in turning your craft into a business. Once you've pinpointed what makes your creations special, it's time to share them with the world. Consider platforms like Etsy or local craft fairs where your work can shine and attract admirers who appreciate handmade artistry.

As you navigate the world of selling, remember that **storytelling** is your ally. Share the journey behind each piece. Customers are drawn to the narrative of your craft, the care woven into each knot. This connection transforms buyers into loyal patrons who value not just the product, but the heart behind it.

Building a business is as much about community as it is about creativity. Engage with fellow artisans, join crafting groups, and attend workshops. These connections can offer support, advice, and even collaboration opportunities. Remember, every successful business starts with a single knot, tied with care and intention.

7.1-Setting Up an Online Presence: Platforms for selling macramé

In today's digital age, creating an **online presence** for your macramé creations not only broadens your audience but also opens up exciting opportunities for selling your handmade pieces. Let's explore some platforms where you can showcase and sell your macramé art.

First, consider **Etsy**, a well-known marketplace for handmade and vintage items. It's a fantastic place for beginners to start because it connects you with a community already interested in unique, handcrafted goods. Setting up a shop is straightforward, and the platform provides tools to help you manage listings and track sales.

Another excellent option is **Instagram**. This visually-driven platform allows you to share photos of your work, engage with potential buyers, and build a following. Use hashtags like **#macramé** or **#handmade** to reach a broader audience. Instagram's integration with shopping features also means you can tag products directly in your posts, making it easier for followers to purchase.

Don't overlook **Facebook Marketplace** for local sales. It's an easy way to connect with buyers in your area who might prefer to pick up items in person. Plus, you can join groups dedicated to macramé or handmade crafts to share your work and get feedback.

Finally, consider starting a **personal website** or blog. This platform gives you complete control over how you present your brand and products. You can integrate an online store, share tutorials, or write about your creative journey, all of which can attract visitors and potential customers.

Remember, building an online presence takes time and experimentation. Focus on platforms that resonate with you and align with your goals, and enjoy the process of sharing your beautiful macramé creations with the world.

7.2 - Growing Your Audience: Attracting followers and potential buyers

Creating a community around your macramé creations can be as rewarding as the crafting itself. As you embark on this journey, remember that your **authentic voice** is your strongest asset. Share your **passion** for macramé through platforms that resonate with you. Whether it's Instagram, Pinterest, or a personal blog, choose a medium that feels **natural** and enjoyable.

Begin by showcasing your work with **vivid, engaging photos**. Capture the intricate details and the beauty of your pieces in well-lit, aesthetically pleasing settings. This visual storytelling draws people in, inviting them to appreciate the craftsmanship and care in each knot.

Engage with your audience by sharing your **creative process**. Discuss the inspiration behind your designs, the materials you choose, and the challenges you overcome. This transparency not only builds trust but also fosters a deeper connection with those who share your love for crafting.

Consider hosting **interactive sessions**, like live tutorials or Q&A segments. This allows you to connect with your followers in real-time, offering them a glimpse into your world and making them feel part of your creative journey. Encourage them to share their own projects, creating a supportive and inspiring community.

Finally, don't underestimate the power of **collaboration**. Partnering with other artists or influencers can introduce your work to new audiences, expanding your reach and influence. Remember, growing your audience is not just about numbers; it's about building meaningful relationships that celebrate the art of macramé.

7.3-Pricing and Marketing Tips: Making your hobby profitable

Turning your macramé hobby into a profitable venture can be a fulfilling journey. Imagine the joy of sharing your **handcrafted beauty** with others while earning from your passion. Let's explore how to make this dream a reality.

First, consider the **unique appeal** of your creations. What sets your work apart? Is it the intricate designs, the choice of materials, or perhaps the story behind each piece? Highlight these elements to attract potential buyers. Sharing the **inspiration and process** behind your work can create a personal connection with your audience.

Next, think about your **pricing strategy**. It's essential to strike a balance between being competitive and valuing your time and effort. Calculate the cost of materials and the time spent on each piece. Don't forget to factor in **overhead costs** like shipping and packaging. A fair pricing strategy not only covers expenses but also reflects the **artistic value** of your work.

Once your pricing is set, it's time to focus on **marketing**. Utilize social media platforms to showcase your creations. Platforms like Instagram and Pinterest are visually driven and perfect for displaying your beautiful macramé pieces. Engage with your audience by sharing **behind-the-scenes glimpses** of your creative process or offering tips and tutorials. This not only builds a community but also positions you as a **trusted expert** in the field.

Consider participating in local **craft fairs** and markets. These events provide an excellent opportunity to connect with potential customers face-to-face and receive immediate feedback on your work. Additionally, collaborating with local businesses can expand your reach. For instance, partnering with a home decor store or a coffee shop to display your work can attract new customers who appreciate handmade art.

Finally, remember that patience and persistence are key. Building a successful business takes time, but with dedication and a genuine love for your craft, you can transform your macramé hobby into a rewarding enterprise. Embrace the journey, and enjoy every knot along the way!

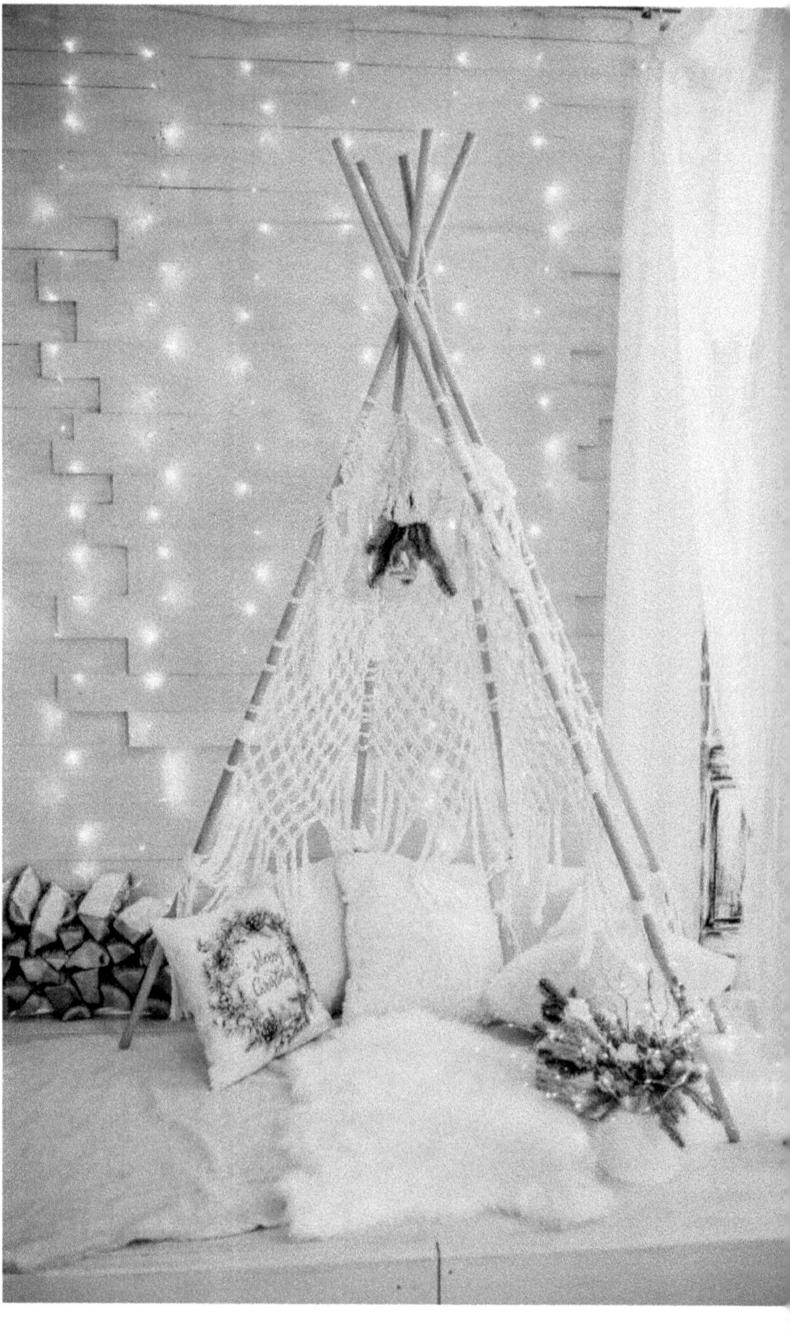

Chapter 8: Creating Practical Macramé Items

As we delve into the realm of practical macramé, imagine the joy of creating items that are not only beautiful but also **functional**. Picture the satisfaction of weaving a macramé market bag, perfect for carrying fresh produce from your local farmer's market. This project begins with a series of simple knots, yet the result is a sturdy and stylish accessory. The rhythmic repetition of knots is like a gentle meditation, allowing your mind to wander and relax.

Consider, too, the elegance of a macramé plant hanger. With just a few basic knots, you can transform a humble pot into a **hanging work of art**. As you craft, envision the lush greenery cascading down, breathing life into your living space. The process is straightforward, yet each knot brings you closer to a piece that enhances your home's ambiance.

Let's not forget the versatility of macramé coasters. These small, delightful projects are perfect for practicing your skills while creating something useful. Imagine the satisfaction of setting a steaming cup of tea on a coaster you made with your own hands. Each knot is a step toward mastery, a journey from beginner to confident crafter.

Through these projects, you'll not only create practical items but also discover the **therapeutic power** of crafting. Each piece you make is a testament to your growing skills and creativity, a reminder that with patience and practice, you can weave beauty into everyday life.

58

8.1-Functional Decor for the Home: Crafting usable decor pieces

Imagine walking into your home, greeted by the warmth and charm of your own handcrafted macramé decor. Today, we'll explore how to transform simple knots into **functional pieces** that not only beautify your space but also serve practical purposes. Whether you're looking to create a cozy corner or add a touch of bohemian elegance, these projects will inspire and empower you.

Let's start with a **macramé plant hanger**. This project is perfect for bringing a bit of nature indoors, allowing your plants to dangle gracefully from the ceiling. Begin by selecting a sturdy cord and a pot that fits comfortably within your chosen design. As you tie each knot, feel the rhythm and flow of the process, letting it guide you to a state of relaxation. The beauty of a plant hanger lies in its simplicity, yet it adds a dynamic element to any room.

Next, consider crafting a **macramé wall organizer**. This piece not only decorates but also declutters, offering a stylish solution for storing mail, keys, or even your favorite magazines. Start with a dowel and some durable cord, and let your creativity flow as you design pockets of various sizes. The result is a unique, personalized organizer that reflects your style and keeps essentials within reach.

Finally, a **macramé table runner** can elevate your dining experience. This project combines elegance with functionality, providing a soft, textured backdrop for your table settings. Choose a neutral cord for a classic look or opt for vibrant hues to make a bold statement. As you weave, envision the gatherings and conversations that will unfold around your handiwork, adding warmth and character to your home.

Remember, each knot you tie is a step towards creating a space that is uniquely yours. Embrace the process, and let your home become a canvas for your newfound skills and creativity.

8.2-Macramé Storage Ideas: Organizers and baskets with style

Imagine transforming your closet space with a touch of artistry. Macramé storage solutions offer a unique blend of functionality and style, turning ordinary organizers into eye-catching decor pieces. Let's explore how you can craft your own macramé baskets and organizers, perfect for adding a personal touch to any room.

Start with a simple macramé basket. Choose a sturdy cotton cord and a hoop as your base. Begin by attaching cords to the hoop using the lark's head knot. From here, you can experiment with different knotting patterns like the square knot or the half hitch, creating a basket that is both robust and beautiful. These baskets are ideal for storing anything from yarn to toiletries, adding a bohemian flair to your space.

For a more structured organizer, consider crafting a macramé wall pocket. Begin by cutting several lengths of cord, and attach them to a wooden dowel using the lark's head knot. Form pockets by knotting the cords together in rows, using the square knot for a tight weave. These pockets are perfect for holding mail, keys, or even small plants, keeping your essentials within easy reach while maintaining a stylish appearance.

Don't forget about the versatility of macramé shelves. By incorporating wooden planks into your design, you can create a hanging shelf that not only organizes but also showcases your favorite items. Use strong, thick cords and secure them with overhand knots to ensure stability. The result is a stunning combination of natural materials and intricate designs, perfect for any room.

With these macramé storage ideas, you can bring both order and elegance to your home. Each piece you create not only serves a purpose but also reflects your personal style, making your space truly one-of-a-kind.

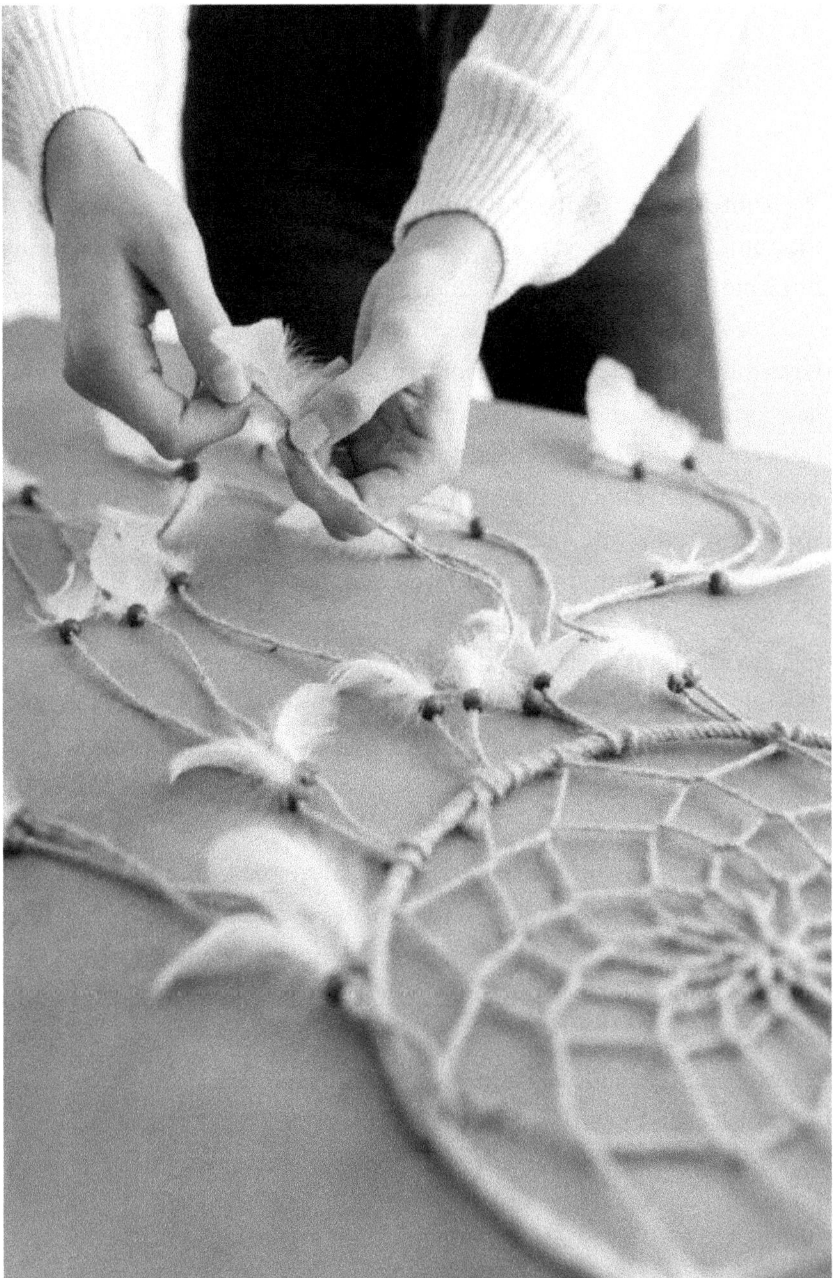

8.3-Everyday Items: Keychains, bookmarks, and placemats

Welcome to the delightful world of creating everyday items with macramé! In this section, we'll explore how to craft **keychains, bookmarks, and placemats**—each a perfect blend of function and style. Let's begin with **keychains**. These small but mighty accessories are fantastic for practicing basic knots while adding a personal touch to your keys or bags. Start by cutting a length of cord, about 30 inches should suffice. Fold it in half and attach it to a keyring using a **lark's head knot**. From here, you can experiment with simple knots like the **square knot** or **spiral knot** to create a design that reflects your personality. Remember, every twist and turn is a step toward crafting mastery.

Next, we move to **bookmarks**. Imagine the joy of marking your place in a favorite book with a handmade creation. Cut a piece of cord around 24 inches long. Fold it and tie a **lark's head knot** around a small metal or wooden ring. From this base, weave a series of **half hitch knots** to form a flat, decorative pattern. The result is a bookmark that's as unique as the stories it holds.

Finally, let's create **placemats**—a practical and beautiful addition to any table setting. Begin with several cords, each about 60 inches long. Anchor them to a dowel or rod using the **lark's head knot**. Use a combination of **square knots** and **alternating half hitches** to build a textured surface. The repetitive motion of knotting can be soothing, transforming each placemat into a meditative project.

With each knot, you're not just crafting an object; you're weaving a story, one that brings warmth and character to everyday life. Enjoy the journey!

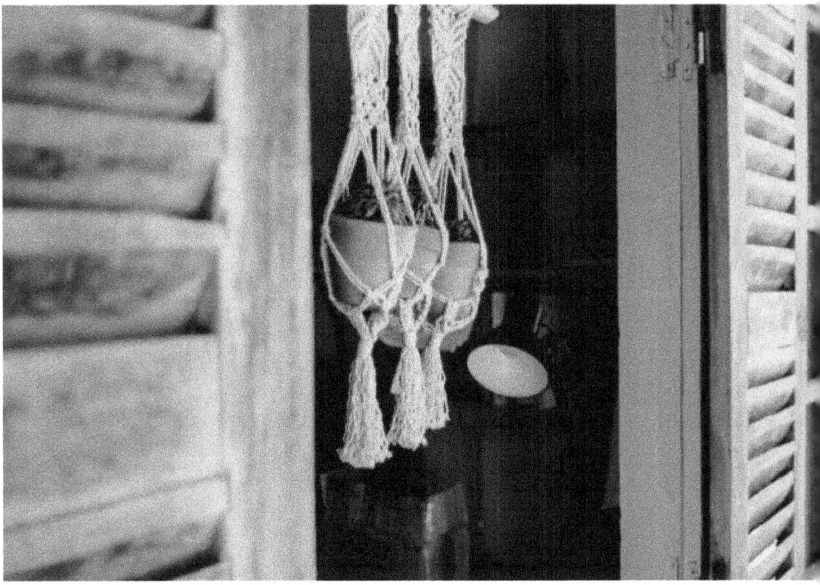

Chapter 9: Beginner-Friendly DIY Projects

Welcome to our journey into the world of **Beginner-Friendly DIY Projects**. Imagine a cozy afternoon, the sun casting a gentle glow through your window, as you settle into your favorite chair with a cup of tea. This is the perfect setting to embark on your first macramé adventure. Today, we'll explore creating a simple yet charming **wall hanging** that will add a touch of warmth and personality to any room.

Begin by selecting a piece of driftwood or a wooden dowel. This will serve as the foundation of your piece, lending it a natural, rustic charm. Cut several lengths of cord, each about twice the desired length of your finished hanging. Remember, it's always better to have a little extra than to run short.

Now, let's dive into the knots. The **lark's head knot** is a wonderful place to start. Fold a cord in half, place the loop over your dowel, and pull the ends through the loop to secure it. Repeat this process with each cord, spacing them evenly along the dowel.

Once your cords are in place, try your hand at the **square knot**. This versatile knot forms the backbone of many macramé designs. Take four cords and use the outer two to tie a square knot around the inner two. With a bit of practice, you'll find the rhythm, and soon your hands will move with ease.

As you work, remember that each knot is a step closer to a finished piece that reflects your unique style. Embrace the process, and let the meditative nature of macramé bring a sense of calm and accomplishment. With each knot, you're not just crafting a wall hanging; you're creating a piece of art infused with your personal touch.

9.1-Handmade Gifts: Crafting thoughtful presents

Imagine the joy on a loved one's face when they unwrap a beautifully handcrafted macramé gift, made with your own hands and heart. Creating **thoughtful presents** through macramé not only allows you to share a piece of your creativity but also adds a personal touch that store-bought items simply can't match.

Let's start with a **simple plant hanger**. This project is perfect for beginners and makes a delightful gift for anyone who loves greenery. Begin by choosing a sturdy, natural cord and a small pot. With a few basic knots, you can craft a charming hanger that will cradle a plant with elegance and style. As you work, remember that each knot is a step closer to a gift that will brighten someone's home.

Another lovely idea is a **macramé wall hanging**. This piece can be as simple or intricate as you wish, making it adaptable to your skill level and the recipient's taste. Select a soft, neutral cord for a classic look, or opt for vibrant colors to add a pop of personality. As you weave the knots, think about the person who will receive it, infusing the piece with your well-wishes and care.

For a more intimate gift, consider crafting **macramé coasters**. These small, practical items are perfect for adding a touch of handmade charm to any coffee table. Use a durable cord and experiment with different knot patterns to create a set that's both functional and beautiful. Each coaster serves as a reminder of your thoughtfulness, making every cup of tea or coffee feel a bit more special.

Remember, the value of a handmade gift lies not only in its beauty but also in the **time and effort** you dedicate to creating it. As you tie each knot, you're weaving a story of care and connection, a narrative that will be cherished long after the gift is given. So, embrace the process, enjoy the creativity, and let your macramé gifts bring joy and warmth to those you hold dear.

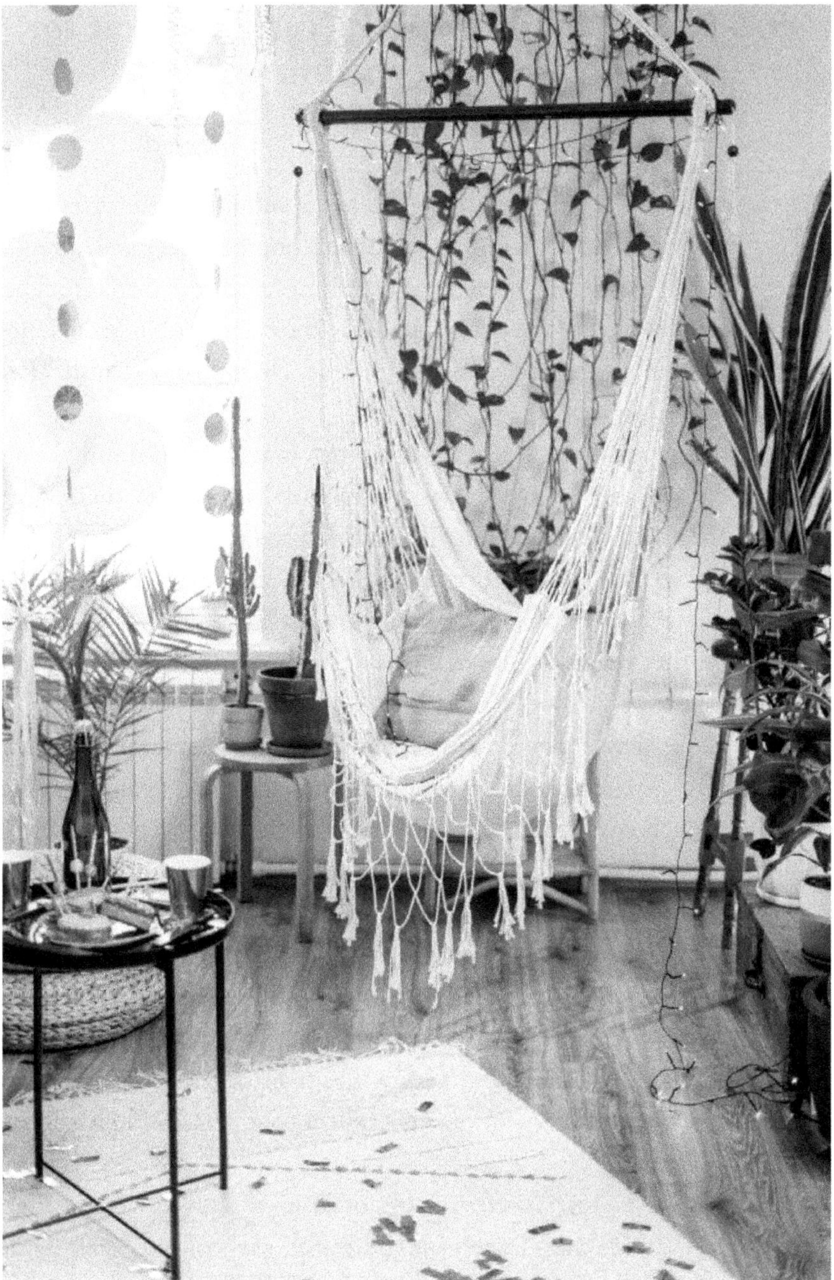

9.2-Holiday and Festive Pieces: Macramé for special occasions

As the holiday season approaches, there's a certain magic in crafting pieces that bring warmth and joy to our homes. Macramé offers a delightful way to infuse your festive celebrations with personal touches that reflect the spirit of the season. Imagine the twinkle of lights dancing off a beautifully knotted garland, or the charm of a handcrafted ornament gracing your tree.

Let's start with a simple yet stunning **macramé garland**. Using natural cotton cord, you'll create a series of basic knots that, when repeated, form an elegant chain. This garland can drape gracefully along a mantel or wrap around your tree, adding a rustic, handmade touch to your decor. The repetition of knots is not just a crafting exercise but a meditative rhythm that allows you to unwind and focus on the joy of creation.

For those who enjoy hosting, consider crafting **macramé napkin rings**. These small, intricate pieces can transform any table setting, adding a touch of elegance and care that guests will surely appreciate. Using a simple square knot, you can create a series of rings that complement your holiday theme, whether it be a cozy winter gathering or a vibrant New Year's celebration.

Finally, let's craft a **macramé ornament**. This project is perfect for using up leftover cord and can be as simple or elaborate as you wish. By combining different knots and adding beads or other embellishments, you can create unique decorations that reflect your personal style and the joy of the season.

Each of these projects offers an opportunity to slow down and enjoy the process of making something beautiful. As you tie each knot, remember that the true gift is the time and love you invest in creating something special for your home and loved ones.

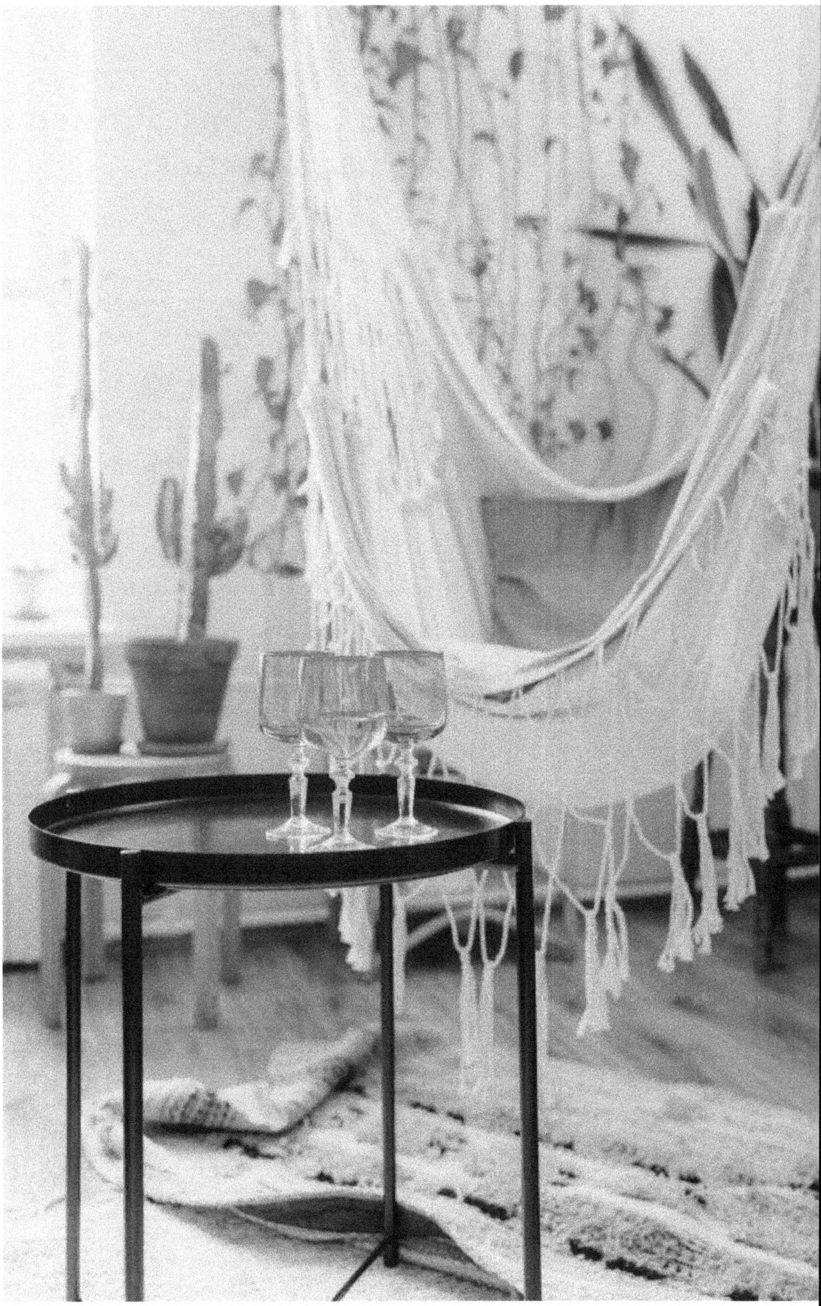

9.3-Easy Outdoor Creations: Projects for gardens and patios

Imagine stepping into your garden, a sanctuary of tranquility enhanced by your own handcrafted macramé creations. These **easy outdoor projects** are designed to add a personal touch to your garden or patio, transforming them into inviting spaces for relaxation and enjoyment.

Let's start with a simple yet elegant **macramé plant hanger**. Choose a sturdy, weather-resistant cord to ensure longevity. Begin by cutting four lengths of cord, each about five feet long. Fold them in half, creating a loop at the top. Secure this loop with a knot, forming the hanger's base. From here, divide the cords into pairs, and start knotting using the square knot technique. As you progress, leave some space between knots to cradle the plant pot snugly. Finish with a strong knot at the bottom, and your plant hanger is ready to adorn your patio with cascading greenery.

Next, consider crafting a **macramé hammock chair**, perfect for lazy afternoons. Begin with a wooden dowel or sturdy branch as the top support. Cut several long cords, folding them in half and attaching them to the dowel with lark's head knots. Use a combination of square knots and half hitch knots to create a net-like seat. Ensure the knots are tight and evenly spaced for comfort and safety. Finish by securing the cords to a second dowel at the bottom, and hang your hammock chair from a strong tree branch or patio beam.

Lastly, a **macramé lantern cover** can add a warm, inviting glow to your evenings. Use a glass jar as the base and wrap it with a net of simple knots, allowing the light to filter through beautifully. Choose a cord color that complements your outdoor decor, and enjoy the serene ambiance it creates.

These projects not only enhance your outdoor spaces but also offer a rewarding crafting experience. Embrace the meditative nature of macramé, and let each knot bring you closer to a serene, personalized retreat.

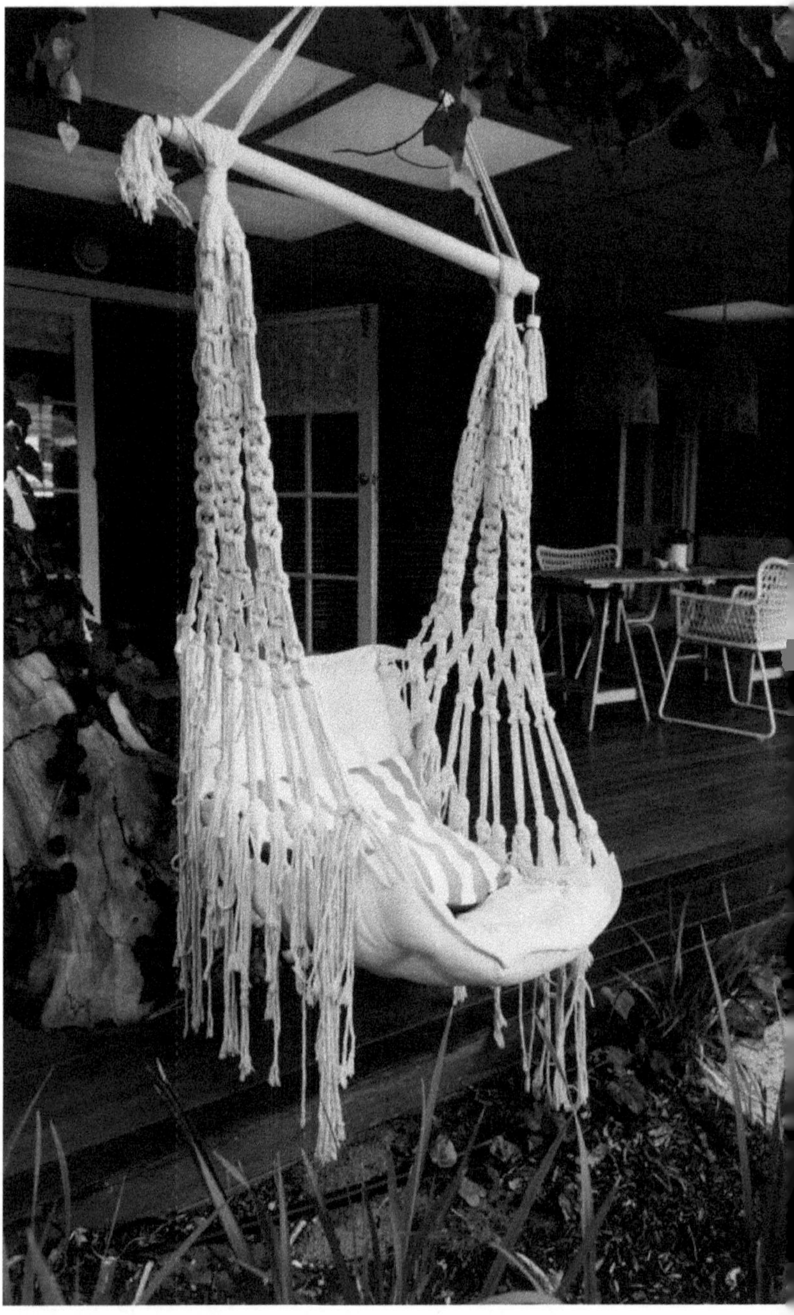

Chapter 10: Crafting Your First Piece in Simple Steps

As we embark on crafting your **first macramé piece**, let's imagine we're sitting together in a cozy workshop, surrounded by spools of colorful cord and the gentle hum of creativity in the air. This is where your journey truly begins. The project we're about to undertake is a simple yet elegant wall hanging, perfect for infusing a touch of bohemian charm into your space.

Start by selecting your cord. Choose a material that feels good in your hands and speaks to your personal style. Whether it's a soft cotton or a vibrant jute, let your instincts guide you. Cut several lengths of cord, ensuring they're long enough to form the intricate knots we'll be exploring. Remember, it's always better to have a bit more than less; you'll find excess cord can be trimmed, but adding more later is a challenge.

With your cords ready, we'll attach them to a sturdy dowel or branch. This is your canvas, the foundation upon which your creation will grow. As you loop each cord onto the dowel, take a moment to align them evenly. This part of the process is akin to setting the stage for a performance; the preparation is as vital as the execution.

Now, let's dive into the **first knot**—the lark's head. This simple, yet foundational knot will secure your cords in place. Visualize the cord as an extension of your fingers, moving with intention and grace. As you pull the cord through the loop, feel the tension and release, the rhythmic dance that is macramé.

With your cords secured, we'll explore the square knot. This is where your piece begins to take shape, where the transformation from cord to art begins. Follow the cord's natural flow, allowing it to guide your hands. Each knot is a step forward, a new layer of your creation's story.

As you work, remember that **imperfections** are part of the charm. Embrace the unique character of each knot, each twist. Crafting is not about perfection but about expression and the joy of creation. Let your hands and heart guide you, and soon you'll have a beautiful piece to proudly display.

75

10.1-Selecting Your Project and Materials

Welcome to the exciting beginning of your macramé journey! As you embark on this creative path, the first step is to **choose a project** that resonates with you. Whether it's a charming wall hanging or a practical plant holder, selecting a project that excites you will make the process more enjoyable. Consider what you want to create and where you envision it in your home. This will guide your choices and inspire your crafting adventure.

Once you've settled on a project, it's time to gather your **materials**. The beauty of macramé lies in its simplicity; you don't need much to get started. The **cord** is your primary material, and choosing the right type is crucial. For beginners, I recommend using a cotton cord, as it's easy to handle and forgiving. The thickness of the cord can affect the final look, so think about whether you prefer a delicate or bold appearance.

Next, consider the **color** of your cord. Neutral tones like cream or beige offer a classic look, while vibrant colors can add a pop of personality to your piece. Feel free to experiment with different hues to match your personal style or home decor.

Don't forget about the **accessories** that might enhance your project. Wooden beads, rings, or dowels can add an extra touch of creativity and functionality. These elements can transform a simple design into something uniquely yours.

Before you begin, ensure you have the right **tools** at hand. A pair of sharp scissors is essential for clean cuts, and a measuring tape will help you maintain precision. You might also find a macramé board or a simple hook useful for holding your work steady.

With your project and materials ready, you're all set to dive into the world of macramé. Remember, this is a journey of relaxation and creativity. Enjoy each knot and the beautiful creation that unfolds in your hands.

10.2-Measuring and Prepping Ropes: Essential setup for success

Welcome to the beginning of your macramé journey! Before we dive into the enchanting world of knots and patterns, it's crucial to get our ropes ready. This step might seem simple, but it sets the foundation for your entire project. Let's make sure you're all set for success.

Start by choosing the right type of rope. For beginners, I recommend using a **cotton cord**. It's soft, easy to handle, and forgiving if you need to redo a knot. Plus, it gives a beautiful texture to your finished pieces. When selecting your rope, consider the **thickness**; a medium thickness is perfect for most projects, offering a balance between sturdiness and ease of manipulation.

Once you have your rope, it's time to measure it. This is where a little patience goes a long way. Generally, you'll want to use a length that is **four to six times** the desired length of your finished piece. This might seem excessive, but trust me, it's better to have a bit extra than to run out halfway through your project. Remember, each knot consumes a surprising amount of rope!

Next, let's talk about **cutting**. A sharp pair of scissors is your best friend here. Dull blades can fray your rope, making it harder to work with and affecting the final look of your piece. As you cut, keep the ends neat to prevent unraveling. If you're working with synthetic ropes, a quick pass of a flame over the ends can seal them nicely.

Finally, take a moment to **organize** your workspace. A clutter-free area helps you focus on the meditative process of macramé. Lay out your ropes, tools, and any other materials you'll need, ensuring everything is within easy reach. This simple preparation can transform your crafting experience into a truly enjoyable and relaxing journey.

10.3-Step-by-Step Assembly: Building your

project from start to finish

As you embark on your macramé journey, remember that each project is a delightful dance of creativity and patience. Begin by laying out your materials in a comfortable, well-lit space. This ensures that you can see each knot clearly and enjoy the process without strain. Take a moment to appreciate the tactile beauty of your cords and the potential they hold.

Start with the **basic knots** you've learned, such as the **lark's head knot** to secure your cords to the dowel or ring. This foundational step is crucial as it sets the stage for the entire piece. Feel free to take your time here, adjusting each knot until it feels just right. Remember, macramé is as much about the journey as it is about the destination.

Once your cords are secured, move on to the **square knot**. This versatile knot will be your trusted companion throughout many projects. As you tie each knot, visualize the pattern emerging beneath your fingers. Allow yourself to fall into a gentle rhythm, letting the repetitive motion become a form of meditation.

As your project grows, you may wish to introduce the **half hitch knot** for added texture and design. This knot is perfect for creating diagonal lines that add a dynamic element to your piece. Pay attention to the tension in your cords; consistent tension will ensure a uniform look.

Throughout this process, remember to take breaks and step back to admire your work. This not only prevents fatigue but also allows you to see your project from a fresh perspective. As you progress, adjust any knots that may have shifted, ensuring your piece remains balanced and true to your vision.

Finally, as you near completion, secure the ends of your cords with a tidy finish. This could be a simple knot or a more decorative option, depending on your preference. Trim any excess cord, being mindful to leave enough for a neat fringe if desired.

With your project complete, take a moment to reflect on your accomplishment. Each knot tells a story of patience, creativity, and the joy of crafting. Display your piece proudly, knowing that you've created something beautiful with your own hands. Embrace the calming satisfaction that comes from turning simple cords into a work of art.

Conclusion;

Thank you for embarking on this journey into the world of macramé! Through these pages, we have explored everything you need to begin and advance in this ancient art, from the basics of knots to more elaborate creations. Each chapter has been designed to make learning easy and enjoyable, allowing anyone from beginners to enthusiasts to immerse themselves in p. We began with an introduction to materials and workspace preparation, essential for concentration and comfort. Next, we explored fundamental knots, such as the square knot and the half knot, followed by intermediate knots, and then combined these techniques into more complex projects. Each section offers visual and detailed guidance to aid the reader and ensure a grateful progression

From decorative designs, such as wall tapestries, to practical and functional ones, such as plant holders and holders, each idea has been selected to inspire your creativity and enrich your home with a personal touch. We have also explored design styles, from bohemian to minimalist, to show you how to adapt macramé to any environment or preference Finally, we have seen how macramé can be not only a hobby, but also a practice of relaxation and awareness, capable of bringing calm and satisfaction. For those who want to turn this passion into a small business, we have included suggestions on how to promote their creations and achieve potential..